Bakthi's Poems and Verses

Author Bakthi Ross

All rights reserved

No part of this book may be reproduced or transmitted
In any form or by any means, electronic or mechanical,
Including photocopying, recording, or by any information
Storage and retrieval system without permission in writing
from the author.

Author Bakthi Ross © 2016.11.17

For information or to order additional books, please write to
Waxwing
PO Box 373
MORAYFIELD 4506
AUSTRALIA
OR PHONE 07-54987214

ISBN   9781922220226

A Creation Without the Creator

A creation without the creator,
A flower without a plant,
As we touch and feel,
We seek that evolutionary power,
There is no God,
Becoming the God is power.

As we understand more,
We create more,
The power of the almighty,
Slowly diminishes.
Then the God will be just a statue.
Your fear of the unknown,
Won't be an unknown creator's power.

A moth imitates a leaf,
As humans we imitate our image as gods.
In our mind there is no God,
Without hands legs and a mind.

A power of creation do not need hands.
The power is the first sense,
Just sensing and reaching,
For that life's necessities

It is like a plant in a dark room reaching for light,
A plant in the desert growing thorns to protect its moisture,
The first evolution could be a spot of pressure,
Then the ray of light and a speck of dust.
How hot and cold pressures,
Made that ray of light and speck of dust,
Into gases, minerals, and acids.

A core rotations and the movements,

Those are the things created life.
Not god.

By Bakthi Ross

<u>Wear Your Own Crown</u>

A crowing crow,
On an empty nest,
A withered tree,
Attracting attention,
Because of the crow's nest.

An awful invasion,
A dancing queen,
Mimicking the crow's song,
The melody is vile,
An insanity of an act,
Is not recognized.

She sings and dances,
Without that sense of reality,
When the melody is in a positive note,
The happy smile on the spiritless person,
is temporary.
When melancholy sets in,
She is back to her mimicking sensation.

Oh! Dancing queen,
Crow is a bird,
The song of crow is only for the crows,
You mimic and mime senselessly,
Why don't you be a dancing queen,
And wear your own crown.

By Bakthi Ross

A Dead Soul

There is darkness beyond your innocence,
A mother is in condemned notion,
A noble quality of a child in question,
A Noddy is dancing in rage,
Oversight of nothingness is a vivid sensation,
Where the child's innocence is seen overtly,
When a dead soul of a wastrel is on parade.

By Bakthi Ross

A Fool's Gold

Senselessness laughter,
That anticipation,
While the girl's name in vain.
Bearing that pain,
That unknown emotion,
Vagueness of that treachery,
The unraveling of a child's innocence,
A tittle tattle of a fool's opinion,
Is like the wound without pain.

By Bakthi Ross

A Python's Prey

A life in an egg,
On a nest waiting to be hatched,
A mother's happiness,
After nine weeks of care,

A fly catcher singing,
A Willy Wag Tail chirping,
And hopping from branch to branch,
Wagging its little black tail.

A twitching mother's eyes,
Caught the wagging black tail,
A menace than a song of a bird,
She could not fly away from her nest,
Leaving the eggs behind.

A python coiled around the tree branch,
With its jaw wide open,
Waited and waited,
No one to chase the snake away.
A disturbed mother's desperation,
To protect her eggs,
Python's tongue slid in and out,
To chase the mother bird away.

She sat on her nest,
And waited for the male bird,
She was reluctant to surrender to a snake,
The male bird was back.

A male bird ten times smaller than the python,
Pecked at the python,
His giant body was no use,
When it was coiled around a tree branch,

A little bird's pecking scared the snake away.

The python moved away looking for another prey,
Free from the preying snake,
Mother bird flew away while the male bird,
Sat and watched the eggs.

By Bakthi Ross

A Little Man's Rant

In search of a prey,
A little man put on a mischievous drama,
He built a mountain out of a molehill,
He silently followed the babblers,

A miser after the mouse's cheese,
A brown moth's malicious intent,
A noddy in a snake's mouth,
Dangling his tail.

Anger is the only thing that makes him act,
A psycho's temper,
A flea in a bag,
And a puma on his trail.

Weak in understanding,
He dances to another one's tune,
His rambling path is the end to his rant,
His elevated feelings only last a while.

Pranks and deceit,
Are his motive,
A caddie without a green,
And golf balls.

By Bakthi Ross

A Senseless Slaughter

The Evilness of a non being,
The cowardness of a sneaky fox,
The treacherous doings of a tramp,
Trembling souls that never sees the truth,
Never coming triumph,
Even though the fool's victory procession,
Includes a Trojan horse.
Dancing clowns,
Smiling Puppets,
A Temporary hype,
When all dies down,
A depressed soul surfaces,
And seeks that temporary hype again,
A senseless slaughter of human emotions.

By Bakthi Ross

A Silent Breath

Sadness and a silent breath,
A final departure,
An atonement of a child,
A bloodless sacrifice,
To catch or to kill a fowl.

By Bakthi Ross

The Long Sleep

When I was a baby I slept most of the day.
When I was a little child I played most of the day.
When I was a teenager I studied most of the day.
When I was in my prime years I worked most of the day.
When I was an old man I read most of the day.
Now I am in my final stage I am back to sleeping all day,
Because I am in training for my long sleep.
I would not have guessed why I slept most of the day in my old age,
But the big man upstairs knows what he was doing.

Bakthi Ross

A Wild Rose

A wild rose between two rugged rocks.
Its thorns are sharper than the English garden rose.
An only flower to smile amongst the dry wild bush.
A red scent amongst the dry twigs.
No butterflies or bees to enhance its beauty.
Wild rose.

Standing alone with its own beauty,
One fresh green leaf and a bud giving hope to the dead bush.
A shining glory.
Keeps the hope alive for the drying grass.
Wild rose.

Bed of roses in an English garden.
Blooms like a young lady's smile.
While the wild rose stands still like an eye sore.
It became harden like a rock rose.
No softness and no affection.
Wild rose.

Its petals taking longer to wither away,
While the English garden rose falls away like the snowflakes.
Heartless and tough.
It was no longer a flower of any means.
It represents a harden women.
Wild rose.

No feelings of love.
If you touch it, it will pierce through you.
It will never be your flower for your valentine.
Its beauty was tarnished by the rugged sense of the bush.
Wild rose.

By Bakthi Ross

Baggages
Baggages are part of one's life journey, when you unload them it will be like the Pandora's Box with dancing angels.
Bakthi Ross

Balless Men!

Withering Pansies,
Dazzling sight,
Daylight robbery,
Unashamed swindling,
Of women's mind,
Dowdle away her time,
Diluted mindless men,
Loiter about,
Rigmarole of her mind,
Petty minded and pitiful existence,
Strain on the world,
Women's intellect is hoarded away,
By feeble men.

Farmer's Love

A trail of cracked mud.
No water, No sheep.
Birds flew away long before the drought set in.
A dusty boot stamping on the ground.

A few dry twigs here and there.
A dame at the verandah, wiping her sweaty face.
A dog curled up sleeping and given up hope.

A day dream is the only thing keeping them going.
If they were birds they would have sensed the long
lasting drought and flown away north.
Now without wings,
And without hope,
Just sitting and staring at the dust flying up
and down on their land.

Dusk is the only time a few smiles and a few conversations
between the dame and the farmer,
She cooked that frozen corn and the peas,
Only green to be seen for miles.

A few glasses of beer do him until morning.
No dreams or worries will wake
him up after that cold beer.

Dawn was like noon,
Started with a scorching heat,
Her man with his dusty boots,
Went around kicking dirt,
He was back on the porch before you know,
Covering his face with an akubra.

No point in looking at the dusty land.

He covered his face and crossed his legs and went to sleep.
Months went by not a cloud to be seen.

Then a sudden loud thunder woke him up.
Black clouds moved faster than water,
Covered the whole land.
At first a few drops of water fell between his dusty boots.
Then the rain turns the land into a muddy pool.

The dame and the farmer stood there in the rain,
Got themselves all wet,
A childish fun between them,
Showered the hope of happiness.

A few days went by,
A green leaf and green grass,
The farmer was back at dawn to work on his farm.
Now his sweat is dust free,
And shone like the smiling green leaves.
Serendipity! A farmer's love was born again.

By Bakthi Ross ©

Sleeping Frog

Green tree frog,
Closed eyes,
Silent dreams,
Moving leaves.

Breathing slowly,
Dab of wet holding the frog on the leaf,
A dandelion smiling on the ground,
Like the wild lady dancing on a stage.

A damsel amazed by the tree frog,
Dawdled around the tree,
Green frog,
Speckled frog,
Tip toe,
Virgin Mary dancing on the meadow.

Bakthi Ross

<u>Children of the Ocean</u>

Dark clouds,
Blinding flashes of lightening,
Blind folded and driven,
Amongst the waves of the sea.

Undisguised shamelessness,
Balmy weather,
Violent waves,
Sailing children of the ocean.

Children carrying their own crosses,
Helpless, walking on a lonely path,
That winds into a life of sadness.

By Bakthi Ross

<u>Crazy Days</u>

The sky is black,
The cloud is moving,
Birds are hiding,
Panic in the homeward bound,
Where people are hurrying and scurrying,
Crowded house,
Calmness is adrift,

Unity of family members in a tender hook,
Cumbersome encounters,
Rising anger,
Crazy days.

Bakthi Ross

<u>Christmas Spirit Still Alive.</u>

I hear that turkey squawking,
I taste that turkey on a platter,
I remember the squabbles,
At my Christmas family reunions,
It supposed to be a happy day,
But we hear all the bad things happened in that year,

Once we stuffed that turkey,
We collectively stuff that happy day,
Emotions run wild,
Our credit bills runs high,
Then we lay our problems on a platter,
Before that stuffed turkey.

We complain about everything,
And everyone,
Then we feel that sheer relief,
It is like the brick wall that had to listen,
To all the problems and complaints.

At Christmas time, our emotional words spin,
Like the jingles on the Christmas tree,
Once we let all the problems out of our heads,
We take the gifts,
And go home in peace,
And look forward to the next one.

The meaning of this happy day is that above,
We flame like the flares on the candle,
And blow off all the burning emotions off our mind,
Like the candles.
Then we go home in peace.

We start the next year like the bright star,
That will lead us into the next peaceful year,
Merry Christmas!
Christmas spirit is still alive.

Bakthi Ross

A Crow's Nest

A crow's nest on a leafless tree,
Is like a dead man's curse,
You can lay eggs on a crow's nest but,
You'll never rear a beauty queen on a crow's nest.

A crow's nest on a leafless tree,
Is a raider's paradise,
An emptiness, a bare mind,
It is postponed to the extent,
That an idiot's babbling mind,
Is like the fallen autumn leaves on the ground.

An empty crow's nest on a leafless tree,
The egg shells of a crow colours the nest,
While the autumn leaves decompose on the ground,
Wild mushroom ready to crop up again,
With the allied knowledge of the original plants.

Bakthi Ross

Dancing Clowns

A lively play,
With puppets and magicians,
Teasing your mind,
Drifting and floating on a black curtain,
Distracting your eyes,
So you see a stuffed bird,

Positions and the way things are placed,
Is an intelligible drama,
Created unrecognizable movements,
A mannequin on parade.

A black cloak,
A scull face,
An amazed audience,
Reduced to despair.

A pigeon with a message,
A rabbit out of the hat,
Bitter criticisms,
Disoriented babbles,
An invisible mockery.

A mouth organ,
A melody of guilt,
Destroys the system,
And throws into disorder.

A clown is off the stage,
His black cloak is on the hook,
An idiot and his ill service,
A squanderer of one's life,
He spun the wool,
Fleeced the sheep,

A quarrel and a controversy,
Behind the black veil.

By Bakthi Ross

Dead Child

Dead silent,
Whizzing wind,
Someone is in dismay,
A tacit emotion,
He walks away,
A white silk covered her face,
No tremor, no thrill,
A silent quivering of singing voice,
That throbbing sound finally departed.

Bakthi Ross

Deadly Influence

Deadly influence bringing up your rear emotions,
The untarnished self-portrait on the mirror,
Now looks disturbed and tarnished,
Oh! Conscience!

Mindless drivel,
Collisions of emotions,
Fear of your own actions,
Reflecting in your mind,
Oh! Conscience!

Uncontrollable urges,
Flashing in the head,
The unthinkable thoughts,
Chain of reflections,
Oh! Conscience!

Can you overcome your own conscience?
That controls you and your mind.

Unholy soul,
Wicked sensation,
Wearing thin,
With that disturbed mind,
Oh! Conscience!

Dethroning that priestly dress,
Hooded cloak,
Falls to the ground,
And you stand in the middle of that cloak,
That once projected you as a saint.
Oh! Conscience!

Bakthi Ross.

Defendless Woman

Sometimes the sky is black,
Sometimes the sky is blue,
When there are clouds,
It covers that smiling brightness of the sky.

Clouded mind and non-smiling face,
Is the wounded self of a human being.
Abused soul of a woman,
Is like a duffer's dancing stage.

He pierces his dagger deeper and deeper,
Into a soul of a defendless woman,
His craving is seeing the sad nymph,
Sitting on a drowning boat.

His smiles are vile,
His appearance is evil,
A soulless tyrant,
Prey on the poor souls.

He satisfies himself like a bully,
His temporary self satisfaction,
Is only last until he demises a woman,
Then he goes with his charitable fake face,
His weak sensation,
You do not need a mirror to see it,
But he goes again after another woman.

He is no man,
He would not face a man,
A coward and only dances under a poor woman's skirt.

A public show he will never do,
In his cowardly cocoon he sits and preys,
Weakest man you'll ever meet,
A saddest being,
He never sees his own true colours.

Anger and madness,
Overpowers his wrong doings,
But he'll never wake up,
Out of his saddest sty,
When you confront him,
He will be defensive and angry.

Depth of the Pain

An emotional pain is a scar that is hard to erase,
It does not surface and disappear,
It takes permanent root in your emotional status,
It is unpredictable,
And it erupts like a volcano when there is pressure.

A man is a murderer,
Because of that emotional scar,
That had never gone away,
His actions are feelingless,
He feels no pain for the murdered victims,
It is an action out of insanity,
He is driven beyond the limit,

Once he had killed a person,
His conscience becomes alive again,
He feels that pain,
He feels sadness,
And becomes a normal person,
Who once had been through sufferings,
That was beyond his control.

Now he seeks to help the others,
Because of his hyper actions reached its peak,
He will no longer be a murderer,
That emotion reached its height,

Bakthi Ross

Disaster Strikes

An inconvenience,
You cannot avoid,
A house washed away,
Nothing! Nothing!
That was all left behind.

You pick up the pieces,
And you move on they say,
But there weren't any pieces to pick up.

A new beginning,
A new place, a new home,
But somehow we replaced everything,
Except our memory,
Our past of that disaster day still lingers on.

To justify the nature's disturbances,
There is nothing,
They say disaster strikes only once in a while,
Now our lives are a disaster every day.

The peace we had,
The routine life we lived,
All disappeared in a moment.

Rotten smell,
Decaying animals,
Muddy paths,
And rotten food.

You could move into a new home,
But you'll never overcome a disaster
that quickly.

We cried
And our tears are dried out,
We let our past wash away,
Now our new beginning,
Has a surcharge.

By Bakthi Ross

<u>Facing Death</u>

A criminal's execution,
A predicted end,
Emblem of morality burnt,
A declining sense.

A final debt notice,
Paid by death,
You walk on a barbed wire cage,
With spikes and thorns,
All sins piercing through you all at once.

Your reflections of your sins,
Lets you make peace with yourselves,
You cannot run or hide,
The whole world is watching the sinner,
He is to be hanged in twenty four hours.

A man in a death row,
His face shows the end,
He begs for mercy,
While the victim of the crime
lay beneath the soil.

Hang! Hang!
The society cries,
While the man in a death row walks alone

in his final steps.

Devil is the only friend,
Who welcomes a man in a death row,
Sardine was his last supper,
And he will be packed and sent away,
A bitter mockery in the last wishing card.

A white rope up above,
A black hood sealed his fate,
He closed his eyes,
And he departs to the devil's zone.

By Bakthi Ross 2012 ©

<u>I Have No Soul</u>

Weight that I carried weighed more than my soul,
I have no soul now,
It is lying flat facing the earth,
It did not go up like everyone else's,
There is no heaven for my soul to rest,
It is on the ground laying parallel to the soil,
Like the dust,
When the wind blows, it flies up,
When the rains falls on it, it comes down again,
I have no soul.

Bakthi Ross

Learn To Lose

A loser's triumph,
Never could be achieved,
He wins one day,
With his foul play.
The next day he is back to his
Losers mourning.

A loser follows his hostage,
He tries for his second minute of satisfaction,
His craving eyes,
His freaky smile,
Is no match for a real winner.

A real loser never could feel,
That satisfaction of losing,
Losing is the first mile stone,
For a winner's final triumph.

You learn to lose first,
Before you could win,
Only person who could survive all the
losing emotions and shame
could feel that victorious winning.

Bakthi Ross

Liar Liar

A thief's dancing emotion,
He tries this and that to fool,
His speech was his fooling sensation,
He speaks like a hyena that waits for the left over carcass,
He preys like a vulture that pulls,

the dead soul like a dead meat,
He is heightened by the parroting lingual talents,
His emotions are at a temporary hype,
He lies and he lies,
Half penny for half a truth,
The halfwit will wear's the crown of hostility,
He is unable to see himself in the hourglass,
He holds a hostage in his mind,
His relentless tries to hide the truth,
He put on this dancing emotion,
No sense of humanity and no sense of peace,
He is a dancing fool and his hyperactive mind,
Only convinces him,
His hypocritical mental outbursts only satisfy him for a minute.
Liar! Liar!

Bakthi Ross

<u>Light of hope</u>

You come out of the earth,
Look for that light of life,
You live for a day,
Died the next day like the mushroom.

Light of life you never see,
All the things you hoped for,
You will never achieve,
You enjoy that moment of fun
and laughter,
In the darkness of that dark
cloud of emotions.

Life seem meaningless,
Without that light of hope,
You live in that darkness,
When you couldn't see that
light of life,
You curled up and die.

Living in the darkness is much better,
Because you do not have to face that light,
You made it dark by crossing that line.
You could never overcome that conscience,
You dark it,
You hide it,
But when you are alone it resurfaces it again.

You feel happy when your mind is clouded,
When your mind is clear,
You hate the world,
You ridicule other people,
You make jokes,
Because you cannot overcome that conscience,

You feel stupid,
You feel fear,
You feel emotionally abused,
Because of that conscience.

You feel scared of life,
Once you felt sorry for the poor,
Now you wish you could kill them all,
Under the cloud of darkness,
You feel anger and hatred,

With the light of hope,
You feel relieved.

By Bakthi Ross

Lonely Souls

Wondering mind,
Nothing to interrupt your thoughts,
It seeks the senses of emotions,
The images are sexually inadequate,
Lonely souls.

Quietness and the blank wall,
Only your imaginations cover the
blankness of that white wall,
It seeks that unwritten, unfeeling sculptures
of a human body,
Lonely souls.

Big and curvy,
Fine features of a human body are not visible,
You feel more than those mare sexual feelings,
You sketch and carve those lonely emotions on paper,
Lonely souls.

You are ashamed of that vivid sensation of sexuality,
But you are intrigued by those indescribable feelings,
Your loneliness brings out those emotions of abnormality,
Lonely souls.

You seek to be recognized,
But your mare self obsessions
stop you from mingling with the norm,

You resort to conquer with your train of thoughts in
writing, drawing and in paintings,
But the society still fails to understand you,
Lonely souls.

Your communication is through your work of art,
They admire and cherish your work,
But they still fail to understand your loneliness of your soul,
Lonely souls.

You walk that lonely roads,
And paint that bare walls,
You fill that blank pages,
Your paces are filled with thoughts of unknown emotions,
Lonely souls.

Bakthi Ross

Man created God. What is unknown and vast is god to mankind. The word God didn't exist until man. The belief in God decreases as mankind find out more about the universe and how it evolved. What is god is whatever beyond human imagination.

Bakthi Ross

Motionless Statue

Tears of sadness,
A teen's misfortune,
And her inexperience,
The connection to that new born soul,
Keeps her going,
If that connection is broken,
She lives with that dead soul,
With no tears or feelings,
She had faced that limit of her strength,
Tested in all forms,
Now she is a mere empty soul that walks,
Her existence is like that rock in the garden,
It never changes form,
It never grows,
Only that little bit of water that lingers,
Makes the moss grow on it,
When the sun shines on it,
It dies again,
With that sharp prickles of the moss,
Protecting her weak soul,
She walks around with a sharp coat of spikes,
But underneath she is an emotionless rock,
You can kick it, you can spit on it,
It feels no pain,
An uncrowned king's conscientiousness refusing to surface,
She no longer scampers,
She is a motionless statue.

Bakthi Ross

Nutty Nancy

Nutty Nancy,
Had nits on her hair,
She pulled at her hair,
And made a knotty tangle,
And it was too hard for her to bear.

She wandered around the park,
With a stick and a bag,
She smelled like cow dung,
And said "Oh! Golly I am a homeless dolly.

When the dog came sniffing around her,
She gave the old bread,
Her plastic bags were not a toy for a stray dog,
She shared the mat with the dog,
And made a home.

Bakthi Ross

Out of Love

I admired him,
I cherished him,
I was in love with him,
He didn't love me,
He ignored me,
I wanted to jump off a cliff and end it all,
Never again I'll fall in love.

A moment of thought stopped me from jumping off a cliff,
I walked alone and couldn't get rid of him out of my mind,
I saw the waves of the sea and it projected the never ending waves of love,
Never again I'll fall in love.

A cup of tea,
A reflection of my face on a tea,
My face moved shapelessly, distorted and deformed,
I couldn't sip the tea and enjoy that moment of love,
I burnt my tongue in that hot tea,
Never again I'll fall in love.

I wrote a song of sadness,
Tears of my emotion rolled down and wet my paper,
Leaching the ink, spots of wet patches on my paper,
With my song written in black,
I couldn't cope, I couldn't confine in anyone,
I was mourning without a dead person,
Never again I'll fall in love.

I sat in silence,
Staring at the sky,
The only star that shined at night,
but I never could reach that star,
The black cloud blocked that shining star,
I am torned, I questioned my own sanity,
I am totally clouded by his mere presence,
But it wasn't meant to be,
Never again I'll fall in love.

I tried to kill myself,
I tried to drown myself,
I wrote stories of sad emotions,
I mingled with the unknown just to shut down the thoughts about him,
I moved to a new place and moved into a new home,
I was angry and I was mad,
I couldn't take any medication for my love sick,

Now I am in a new place.

After all those painful emotions,
My pain of love moved away from me,
I am out of love,
Never again I'll fall in love.

By Bakthi Ross

<u>Playing With Fire</u>

Flames of fire,
That I desire,
Wild fires,
Bush fires,
I make them ignite,

When I see that flame,
My face shines in that light,
I smile, I enjoy that flaming moments,
Then I go back again to set that fire again,
I am the flamethrower.

Fire! Fire! They cry,
That is the echo I liked the most,
They panic, they cry,
As I watched them burn.
Now I am caught in my own fire,
And I could not get out of that fire,
I cried, I panicked,
As my desire died with me.

I no longer be here,
To conquer that desire,
Well lit, well burned,
I am now part of that fire.
I would shine no more,
I am black as tar,

And cooked as charcoal,
I say goodbye,
Because I was burnt alive,
Flames! Flames! Well lit flames.

Bakthi Ross

<u>Pressure Cooker</u>

Mountains of hurdles,
Baggages of the past,
You carry it alone,
If the worm sticks its head out,
The preying birds will eat it.

People live in a cocoon of emotions,
When the commotion starts,
Anger, frustrations, hatred and all sort of emotions,
Whirls like a tornado,
And throws things out of the whirl.

Distress, mental pain and pressure,
Calms down and come to a standstill,
Only the big empty hole it leaves behind in your cocoon,
And you are out,
And flying like a butterfly
With flying colours.

Bakthi Ross 2011

See Yourself In A Framed Picture

Mourn for that loss,
Yearn for that happiness once you have had,
Loss is such a painful emotion,
It drains you off your desires of life,

You cry,
You sit in silent,
You watch that pictures,
And enjoy that past moments,
Then the tears run out of you,
Like the rolling pearls of emotions.

That picture you carry in you,
And in your mind carries you over that
hurdles of life.

Loss is a picture of an emotion,
You picture yourself in a framed painting,
You colour your background,
You let that light shine through the darkness,
You draw over the ups and downs of the landscape,
You let that water flow over those difficult rocks,
When you finished that picture,
It reflects all the emotions of that framed loss.

Once you are out of that framed picture,
You can see the clear picture of yourself,
Now you can move on to the next picture
of your life.

By Bakthi Ross

Shielded By Mud
Dedicated to Mr William Ross

Stuck in a ditch six feet deep,
I could hardly stick my head out to look,
After the rain there were puddles of water,
Every time a soldier passed by,
He would splash me with muddy water.

Some days I looked like I was made of clay,
We couldn't tell anyone off,
We couldn't provoke anyone,
Keep the tempo down,
and tolerating everything was important.
I sat there grinding this scrap metal,
But I was interrupted by soldiers walking back and forth,
Some sat there and wrote a letter,
Some played their little harmonica,
He had to play it so quiet,
You could hardly hear the tune.

Our week old sweaty shirts and pants,
Sometimes we could hardly cope with our own smell,
It was like the shanty town in Hongkong,
The dirty water had nowhere to run,
Too many sweaty bodies slept in a ditch.

We could hardly walk in the narrow ditch,
Without our shoulders rubbing against each other,
Some stared at their family photos for hours on end,
Waiting is hard in a normal situation,
It was even harder at war times.

I occupied myself with this scrap metal,
While our bodies were left behind like the scrap,
Some made it home and some didn't.

When they were blown to pieces,
You could see the hands and legs flying in the air,
Hardest part was leaving the mate behind and walking off,
The image of those dead eyes I never could forget,
Some went back and closed the eyes off the dead bodies,
Some just had to leave and run,

I sat there and grinded,
The scrap metal to keep the tension down,
No one would speak about anything that had happened,
If you lose a mate no one said nothing,
They continued like nothing had happened.

When we went to India,
None of the Indians wanted to sit with us,
We smelled like cattle and we ate beef,
They didn't like us eating their god,
So they backed away.

Now I am at home,
I still couldn't overcome my emotions,
Whenever I talked about the war,
My wife left the table,
She couldn't take it anymore.

By Bakthi Ross

The Air In Motion

There are no rain drops without wind,
There are no rainbows without wind,
Water will be thrown on you
like it is coming out of a bucket without wind,
Clouds do not move without that wind,
The air in motion,
And the sound of that blowing,

Winds up the motions in everything,
When it slow and fresh we enjoy that motion,
When it is wild and roaring,
We hide from that noxious power,
It will wind us down or sometimes it will wind us up,
We could not live without that wind,
Even though we look for that wind breaker.

Bakthi Ross

The devil! The decider!

A coffin only contains your body,
Your soul departed a long before,
A wooden brown box,
Empty as your body,
No life, No soul.

The beauty of the coffin,
The craftsmen's delight,
Polished and made the coffin shine,
Your body once shined,
Now in a brown box ready to decay.

No one, all alone,
Lay in a brown box,
No dream except the devil,
Waving his spear,
And pulling you.

You didn't plan before death,
Your sins and your good deeds,
Measured by the devil,
Devil is the decider,
You'll not meet the god,

Until you reach heaven.

By Bakthi Ross

<u>Flow of Water</u>

Water flows,
Over rocks and over the sand,
Waves of light reflecting through the water,
Changes shape according to the unevenness of the ground,
Flow of water.

It runs over slopes,
When it encounters a mount it stops and puddles,
It spins in a puddle yet it cannot escape,
Flow of water.

It slithers like a snake,
Pulls you down with it like a magnetic force,
It stops at nothing until it reaches the big sea,
Flow of water.

Sea of water,
Movements of waves,
Reaches the shores but cannot conquer,
Back to the seas but will be back again for another try,
Flow of water.

Sea rises and sand erosions,
A feelings of a conqueror,
But still slips away,
Like the flow of water,
Flow of water.

Relentless tides,

Keeps reaching the shores,
When I conquer,
There won't be anything but thin air,
Flow of water.

Wet and dry,
Winds and waves,
Ups and downs,
Life flows whether there is a mountain or a mole.
Flow of water.

Waves of strength,
That pushes you over the hill,
When there is a low tide,
The calmness of the water,
Gives you that satisfaction of relief,
But how long could it last,
Flow of water.

The strength of big waves,
Overpowers our emotions,
Yet again we relentlessly try the same motions.
We push and we pull,
Sometimes it breaks and sometimes it flows away.
Flow of water.

We don't really recognize the flow of our emotions,
It comes in low tide high tide and waves of succession,
It is a cycle of power,
One wants over another.
Flow of water.

By Bakthi Ross

The Last of Her Tears Meets the Black Sea.

Darkest cloud,
Darkest day,
Her darkest moment,
Accepting Reality,
No black veil,
Ben is behind bars,

Black swans floating,
Over a black sea,
A helpless mother standing alone,
While her tear drops reached the end.

Bakthi Ross

The Nerve We Have

The nerve,
It has a predefined path,
When you knock on it,
It breaks that connection,
When you keep knocking on it,
It totally changes form.

Without that nerve you have no conscience,
Without that nerve you have no emotion,
Without that nerve you have no predefined human form,
Without that nerve you are more like a vegetable
than a smiling norm.

The changed nerve sometimes creates that super human,
Sometimes it creates an animal,
Sometimes it creates an abnormal being,

We can change the path of a human nerve,
And it will lead to the evolution of all creations,

We consider ourselves as a super being,
Above animals, above aliens, above all creations,
That sixth sense is tarnished, improved and improvised,
To enter that new world, that new planet,
That new form of being,
The nerve we have.

Bakthi Ross 2011

The Painting

The painting I see,
The beauty of the picture I feel,
The fall of the colours,
The darkness of the shades,
When I see the painting close,
I feel the drooping drops of paints,
When I see it from a distance,
I feel the beauty of one's
Expression.

Bakthi Ross

Changing Flags

The past I don't want to know,
The future I do not know,
The flag that is bare,
Represents no country or a man,
I have respect for my flag,
But if it changes like the weather,
Its representation is worthy of none.

By Bakthi Ross 2010

White Coffin

A child lay in a white coffin,
A procession to the burial site,
A sadness,
A black veiled woman,
Walked slowly,
As her tears fell to the ground after each step.

A hooded man's sin,
A shadow followed the burial procession,
As he hid behind the tree,
His black eyes with sadness said good bye to his victim.

A few seconds of reality awakens the hooded man,
He felt that he had sinned,
As he walks home alone,
And he loses that state of mind again,

He is back to his rituals,
He put on his hood,
Walks alone in that lonely path,

Until he preys again.

By Bakthi Ross

Why I Write

My mind is clear,
My thoughts are pure,
My flow of thoughts flows well
when I am alone,
It moves like a cloud,
And runs like a river,
I hold on to those thoughts,
Because I enjoy it most,
When I put it in writing.

I write because I can relive those moments,
I write because I can create something new,
I write because I fill that blank pages,
I write because my writing becomes a work of art,

My emotions,
My senses,
My feeling,
All flows on a page like a story,
Like a poem,
Like a verse.

Because without the pen and a paper my thoughts
and my imaginations will disappear forever.

Bakthi Ross

YOU CANNOT BE SERIOUS

Changing sky,
Changing clouds,
Changing days,
You cannot be serious,
Time would stay still for you.

Changing seasons,
Changing leaves,
Changing flowers,
You cannot be serious,
Time would stay still for you.

Changing seas,
Changing tides,
Changing waves,
You cannot be serious,
Time would stay still for you.

Changing water,
Changing rain,
Changing rivers,
You cannot be serious,
Time would stay still for you.

Changing moon,
Changing light,
Changing night,
You cannot be serious,
Time would stay still for you.

Changing people,
Changing lives,
Changing places,
You cannot be serious,

Time would stay still for you.

By Bakthi Ross

A Wrinkled Old Face

A wrinkled old face,
Seen the days of ups and downs,
He sat there day after day,
Year after year,
Looking at the same people,
And the same scenery.

A face in the crowd,
That never changed the scene,
Same place, Same crowd,
His thoughts occupied his mind,
In such a way,
You couldn't even see him,
Blink his eyes.

Such a stare you could only,
See on a dead body,
He was weary of life,
Even if you drop dead in front of him,
He would not move.

A pain, a merciless hardship,
He would have suffered,
Only the wrinkles on his face,
Was his evidence.

He was a cross-bearer,
He suffered for his own belief,
When a little kindness shown by anyone,

His partly open mouth made a little smile,
Like he had no strength to smile.

To weep he had no tears,
To cry he had no voice,
He would fade away,
But his memories kept him alive,
In the hope of change,
A face in the crowd,
A wrinkled old face.

By Bakthi Ross

Meaningless Talk

Deeply discreditable,
Scandalous,
Lacking in shame,
One man's guilt.

Ridiculous talk,
Conscience of guilt,
Never stoppable short comings,
I account for nothing,
My payment of my due is my abuse.

A ruthless abuse,
An unbearable defeat,
It was fun once,
Now it is an uncontrollable anger.

I fight, I thrash,
I strike, I beat,
My battering is in the frying pan,

Flapping like a pancake.

I conceal my jealousy,
I conceal my anger,
My strength is sitting on a heavy dark cloud,
I stray away from my own pain and sufferings,
But I do not have a resolution.

I panda, I pretend,
Until, I get a response,
An unfeeling hard stone I'd be,
When the bird is in my hand.

My meaningless talk is my peace,
I could never overcome who I am on a stage,
I blather away my time,
When I stop I blaze like a fire,
And display my anger.

When I am face with my victim,
I shrivel like an innocent child.

By Bakthi Ross

Shining Stars Always Fades Away

Shining stars always fades away,
A triumph,
A glory,
A trophy,
Until the next one's triumph,
It will shine.

One's hope,
One's achievements,
It is like the sun in the sky,
It rises and sets,
Shining stars always fades away.
A golden trophy never fades,
But the inscriptions on the trophy,
Has a space,
To add another winner,
Shining stars always fades away.

By Bakthi Ross

<u>To Be Collected</u>

A body,
A black bag,
A tag with an unknown name.

A traced relative,
Never met the dead person,
He's to collect the body for burial.

Lived alone,
Dead alone,
No one ever phoned,
No one ever visited.

Now an unknown soul,
Collected by a stranger,
He would be buried alone.

Because of the last name,
A last goodbye was given,
A last respect only comes,

When you are dead.

If you are alive and knew,
You would be in a black bag to be collected,
You would have called,
Or made an arrangement for your burial.

Somehow we do not think about death,
When you are lonely you are scared of death,
Being lonely and being alone is a death in a living form.

To be tagged,
To be collected,
You feel as though the package that was not,
Delivered to the right owner.

By Bakthi Ross

The Future of Our Progress

We decorate you with medals and stars,
But your shine will fade away.

Memory lingers,
As you fade,
Its shine loses its emotional value.

A brave soldier's victory through bravery,
Wisdom through his service,
We fought for this and that,
As time passed,
We have to fight for new things,
That hasn't got the old value.

Old days were good,
These days are bad,
Why? Because we haven't got that,
Emotional value today.

No customs,
No cultures,
No emotional values,
Once some things were morally wrong,
Today they are meaningless.

The future of our progress,
Have no attachments to human souls.

By Bakthi Ross

THE DEVIL'S INSANITY

Quieten the quarrelsome,
Award the un-suppressable,
Pardon the wrong doers,
Harm the mischievous,
Mislead the trustworthy,
Doubt the un-doubtable,
Misuse the gullible,
Barricade the rebellious,
Imprison the innocent,
Halleluiah to the devil.

By Bakthi Ross

Only One Mourner

Wild oaks,
Falling leaves,
A man in a black cloak,
Riding a horse with a cart.

A raven's deep flight,
A raw sense,
A poor performer,
Guiding the horses.

An ill behaved girl's drama,
On a lonely road,
A Quaker on the prowl,
With a scroll of sacred words.

A preacher in a church,
A body in a coffin,
A long drawn out sermon for a prisoner,
And a pittance for the priest.

The man in a black cloak,
Bow to the dead body,
Only one mourner,
For the dead nobody.

By Bakthi Ross

A Desperate Plea

Hands up,
Pulling current,
A sound of desperation,
Barely heard,
Violent waves,

Pulling down the life of a soul.

A check mate,
An undeniably cornered situation,
A way out is,
A suicide note,
A drowning of not facing shame.

Dead! Dead!
Drowned! Drowned!
Permanently silenced,
No questions asked,
Re-direction of truth.

Society in mourning,
While the fox of prey,
Shields the true picture with a black curtain.

A history was made they said,
But it is all a matter of time,
Time will tell the truth,
To be in a position of difficulties,
| When the two lines meet.

A body not found,
A decomposing body in water,
Sharks ate the flesh of the highly esteemed.

An effigy distorted,
Like the moving water,
Faded away from the center of the,
Contemptible circle.

By Bakthi Ross

Queenslander

A tall roof,
Wooden verandah,
Sitting on a rocking chair,
Watching the birds.

Summer heat,
Homemade lemonade,
A sip of cool breeze,
A calming gas in a hot fire.

Heat waves,
Mirages of expectations,
Nothing will change the summer heat,
We wear it and we sweat it.

Queenslander,
Tanned and tough,
Dusty boots and checkered shirts,
Akubra off the head,
To cover the face from the heat.

A midday sleep,
An unwanted wait,
The nature's rest,
Leaves craving in thirst.

A moving sun,
A following shadow,
Brings back the evening breeze,
Queenslander off again,
To work until dusk.

Queenslander is the name,
That moves with the season,

You cannot bend or break,
Without the sun's order.

He sleeps until dawn,
And moves with the sun,
A Queenslander.

By Bakthi Ross

A Face in the Crowd - 2

Two dark black moving eyes,
Agitated,
Reluctantly looking around,
A slight nervousness creeping through,

His final moments,
A suicide bomber,
He was dying for his belief,
Martyrdom is more valuable,
Than living like a loser.

He was moving around the crowd,
Neatly dressed,
He was dressed for his funeral,
No one looking at him as a suspect.

He wants to go with the crowd,
He wants to die with the enemy,
I am taking some with me he whispers,
He wasn't going to change his mind,
Even though life offered more.

His determined mind,
His anger,
He feels the injustice,

One man's power,
If you are willing to die,
There are no other power above it he says to himself.

He was willing to let go of his life,
Just to get a little bit of revenge,
Eye for an eye,
Man for a man,
I am paying my due he sighed.

He blows himself amongst the crowd,
He didn't die alone,
He had done his duty,
Whether heaven welcomed him or not.

Bakthi Ross

He Didn't Find Love

The sky was grey,
His tears at bay,
A maiden's smile,
Never to be found.

Lifeless feelings,
No love affairs,
A black day,
A rocky path.

No love,
No warmth,
An attraction seeks,
In one's mind.

A star in the sky,
An unreachable light,

It didn't shine,
In his craving heart.

Dreaming and imagining,
But he didn't find love,
A lonely life without,
Anyone's love.

A harden heart,
He was tough,
But now and then,
Other's emotions of love,
Made him smile.

True love he had never found,
A screen in front,
He hid behind,
A shielded emotion,
A deprived life.

A lonely soul,
Without love,
Strayed on to,
Lean on a dead vine,
Love eluded him.

Bakthi Ross

To Be In Exile

To be born in a country,
The soil gives you the sense of belonging,
That builds the devotion towards the country.

To be in exile,
You are bring to bear the donkey,

The sense of belonging,
You have carried from your womb,
Will not let you settle down.

A flag of your country,
Is the strength of the people,
The song of the nation is the voice.

As a single person you are part of a tree,
With roots, flowers and fruits,
When you blossom like a flower,
And bears the fruits of the society,
Your nation will prosper.

When an individual is unhappy,
It spreads onto the society,
It creates behind the scene plots,
To demise the society.

If the society is happy,
The country will go forward,
It is not what you do for your society,
It is what you do for yourself,
Will makes the society prosper.

When an individual is happy,
And satisfied in his endeavours,
His achievement will spread onto the society.

An encouraging word,
While you are in exile.

Bakthi Ross

An Unmentionable Author

A gentle soul,
Quietly spoken,
Proper English,
And proper manners.

He moved away from his homeland,
Dare he loses his mother tongue,
Years went by,
Literatures changed,
But his classy language stayed with him.

He was an author,
Wrote literary novels,
He wrote day and night,
When he read his story,
There was a silence in the room,

His high standard of English,
That's what made them quiet,
They listened quietly,
Most immigrants looked up to him,
His class and aristocracy,
Stood with him until the end.

Africa to Australia,
Papua New Guinea to Fiji,
India to China,

His status was recognised,
When he spoke in that gentle manner,
An inspiration he was!
Always giving that helping hand.

Bakthi Ross

An Accidental Event

A root, a start,
An unknown seed,
A power of conditional release.

Creation has no power,
Creation is what you know,
If God created everything means,
He would have known,
What he was going to create,
He would not have said "Heaven and Earth,"
Because Earth is part of heavenly bodies,
Part of the solar system,
Evolution is what you don't know.

Power of evolution is non-existent,
Because it is an accidental event,
Why life evolved is to,
Cope with the conditions.

A pressure inside,
Pops up as a life outside,
A leaf is needed for a tree to exist,
It absorbs and releases.

A rotation collects things,
And created heat and gases,
Each element reacts and releases,
When they are out of the soil,
They face the conditions outside,
Sun, oxygen and so on,
To suit the conditions, it forms leaves,
Then a flower,
Then a fruit to be in a cycle of life.

A shape of a leaf,
Is an ending,
It is a limit of gases, acids and minerals,
Come out to face the conditions.

A reaction of acids forms patterns of things,
Shapes of leaves are,
Like jumping gases and acids,
They go like bubbles, waves and strings.

A leaf grows no further,
A flower turns into a fruit,
It is the stages of process,
That created different species.

Bakthi Ross

Smell of Death Marigold

I am partly burnt,
And I am partly lost,
I walked half way,
But I cannot jump,
Smell of death marigold.

My flesh was cooked,
I can smell death,
I watched the people from a burnt window,
They watched me as I was burnt alive,
Smell of death marigold.

People were falling,
Fire was burning,
I cannot comprehend the pain I am was going through,
As I slowly burnt to death,

Smell of death marigold.

Yelling and screaming,
Piles of burnt bodies,
Black was the colour of smoke,
That clouded the whole building,
Smell of death marigold.

You cannot move,
You cannot rush,
You cannot jump,
Every entrance was full of people,
Pushing over each other,
My life over yours, your life over mine,
Smell of death marigold.

Legs were torn,
Hands were blown,
Children were helpless,
Men are speechless,
Screams of desperate women,
Burning hell,
Smell of death marigold.

Burning flesh,
Burning building,
There was a roasted dog lay beside the entrance,
I am the next cooked roast to be tabled,
I am in pain, and I am facing death,
Smell of death marigold.

Kill the vandal, Curse the culprit,
Spare a thought for the innocent,
If all were culprits, society would not work,
I was put out like the fire that was burning in me,
Save the society! Save the world!

I have faced the end of my problems,
Smell of death marigold.

At my last minute I call for the god,
I confessed to all my sins,
I yearned for my children and I called for my wife,
I wanted to see them one last time,
One eye is gone, I am still partly alive,
I have seen life, now I have seen death,
Good bye world! I hope your problems will end one day,
Smell of death marigold.

I cannot compensate,
For the violence some people create,
I saw the hell of fire,
Until my eyes were burnt,
Smell of death marigold.

Firey colour marigold,
Fire was my death marigold,
I am gone, my remains are no use.
Smell of death marigold.

Bakthi Ross

A Swaggie's Dream

A lone wanderer,
A sacred sense of freedom,
Incapable of submitting to pitiful orders,
To be out of the society's jungle,
I wander into the open world.

Flying birds,
Buzzing bees,
Silky white clouds,

An the smiling sun,
A sacrifice just to be free.

A sack and a dog,
A strength and penance,
A blowing wind,
That wipes away the memories.

After seeing the vastness,
And the wealth of the world,
I found peace,
And let go of the tuppence that was not worth having,
My twiddling thumb,
I lay on the grass and watch that unlimited happiness.

I struggled, I scuffled,
But in the dark sky the stars shines again,
I walk miles and miles,
While my sweat soaking my shirt,
I talk and I sing,
It is my own tune I enjoy.

No orchestra,
Only the sounds of the birds and the bees,
I am cut off from the society,
But my own feet and my freedom,
Carried me through that open land.

My peace is genuine and permanent,
No commotion, no turmoil,
I am that little shoot on a bush,
But I smile like the tall gum tree.

No execution, No gallows,
But for the two faced,
Here are my two pennies,

The unattested justice,
And the ultra motive,
Was the beginning of my journey.

Now I am unstressed,
And unacceptable,
But I am unaffected,
By the worldly desires.

By Bakthi Ross

<u>A Soldier Never Dies</u>

A loyal soldier,
A honourable job,
A medal for his heroism,
A noble deed,
He was wrapped in his patriotic flag.

He was dead in flesh,
And died in our hearts,
A monuments of memories,
A soldier never dies in our soul.

A statue,
A stability of emotion,
A quality of action,
A victory medal,
A soldier never dies.

A responsibility in once shoulder,
A victory flag of a nation,
We cheer,
We cherish,
A soldier never dies.

A celebrated fame,
An achievement,
A hero,
An unforgettable courage,
A soldier never dies.

By Bakthi Ross

<u>Falling Leaves 2</u>

A life,
A sense,
An expectation,
It grows,
It flowers,
It fruits,
Then it falls like the falling leaves.

Death is an end,
But for falling leaves,
It had to give life to the new,
To fall in right places,
Against the moving wind,
Like the falling leaves.

To part from the family tree,
It is the isolation,
That evokes the imagination,
Like the falling leaves.

You cannot restrain,
You cannot control,
A powerless performance,
A continuous cycle,
Like the falling leaves.

You stop,
You stare,
But for the falling leaves,
Autumn comes in a cycle of things,
Like the falling leaves.

An oak leaf on the ground,
A star in a process,
It turns gold in colour,
Before it deminishes,
Like the falling leaves.

By Bakthi Ross

Ha! Ha! Butterfly

I fly like a butterfly,
I utter and titter like I am on cloud nine,
When I wake up,
Birds were chirping,
But I had no words to mutter.
I look at the day, I wait for the night,
I am here to prey I think,
Then I put on a bird call,
My gimmicks and my new image,
Attracts no prey,
I am getting old I suppose,
But the days I had were good.

I am in my fifties,
I relied on thrifties,
I suppose I have to pull my socks up,
And let go of this fantasy life.

Friends are only there when they want something,

They come and go,
But I made them all look at their life,
Their past is the one I am mostly interested,
Because there is no future for some,
By the time they wake up,
I said to them "Dido," I ruined your life.

I do not care what they want or what they understood,
I put on a drama, whether there were any audience or not,
I imagined, I dreamed,
And I believed strongly on the things of the past,
I believe in the things that are suitable for me,
It is me! It is me! I please after all.

I imagined I can make them envy of me,
I walk and talk like I have a chip on my shoulder,
My emotional rollercoaster kept me insane,
But then again it is all my imagination.

There are no second chances in life,
But if they gave me one chance I'll wreck it again,
Because I like to be on cloud nine all the time.

So don't be a butterfly,
Because when the wind blows you would not be able to fly,
When the night comes you would not be able to see,
So be an earthworm and munch on all the scraps,
And make a mountain out of a molehill.

Bakthi Ross

Weak Minded

A friarbird follows a maid,
Dragging her feet, blisters on her toes,
She was reaching for the sky,
While the mandolin was played by a Madonna.
It was a shameful act of a relentless tyrant,
A slip knot around the neck of a hanged man,
The dangling feet and the drooping neck,
It was the only thing that satisfy the sense of a sourpuss.

Her relinquished hopes are her belief,
His lost remains are her victory,
His resigned soul was an escape from himself,
His lagging strength was her power of control.
His temporary calmness was only when he could feel,
A parson's last prayer was her parting gift.

By Bakthi Ross

Words Of War

I am barely seventeen,
I did not understand the world,
I did not understand war,
I went to war,
Can you believe it?

I dug ditches,
I stayed in wet clothes for days on end,
My face was covered in mud,
My finger nails were black as tar,
I fought the war without any emotions,
Can you believe it?

When my mate was blown to pieces,
There weren't any remains to be buried,
They said "He was missing in action,"
Can you believe it?

I took up smoking,
And sat on muddy puddles,
I picked up scrap metals,
Used any tools and made a cigarette lighter,
That was how I passed my time,
While I was waiting in the ditches,
Can you believe it?

My contribution conquered the world,
But I remained a corporal,
Can you believe it?

By Bakthi Ross

Laughter

Laughter is an emotion that spreads,
Like the yawning,
If you laugh I laugh with you,
Whether I understood it or not,
What you are laughing about,
When you yawn I yawn after you,
Because it is catchy and spreads,
If you see a picture of a laughing person,
Your emotion changes to a happy state,
And you laugh with them.

The Sealed Box of Life

I am a bit stiff,
I had a bit too much the night before,

I had seen the life through my watery eyes,
It was not as clear as the crystal.

I am in my last days,
I still could not see life as a clear cut journey,
I am in my eighties,
I enjoyed it to the full,

I have no regrets in leaving,
This flight of life,
I am ready to open my Christmas gift box,
While they are ready to shut my,
Box of life's journey.

This may be my last Christmas,
I want to enjoy it,
I hold on to my present,
I could hardly undo the ribbon,
It is tied in knots,
I had a bit too much,
And I sat there staring at it like a lost soul,

My mind is in knots,
My bones cracked like the Christmas crackers,
I am eighty eight,
I enjoyed every moment of my life.
I had it good! I had it bad!
I am on my way to heaven,
I say Merry Christmas and a Happy New Year!
Hold on to the gift of life,
It is worth opening it.

By Bakthi Ross

Headless Tramp

Arrows of accusations,
Whining notions,
The last drink of the blood,
The live sacrifice,
Drooping neck,
Lacking vitality,
The last breath,
The warm air,
The dancing soul,
Departed from your lifeless body.

Closed eyes,
No connection to anyone or the world,
Lying still the cold body,
Relentless scrutiny,
He lost his flight,
On the words of a liars scheme.

No morals,
No compassion,
A lunatics mental babbles,
Constant pressure,
Finally succumb to the pressure,
Peace he seeked,
And departed to the heavenly peace.

There weren't any truth in the lunatic's babbles,
But it pestered on and on,
You cannot tell a stupid person,
To seek the truth,
It is a headless scum,
A treacherous snake.

It will trap you in an emotional rollercoaster,

No rational in its babbles,
But it mutters day and night,
Like a raving maniac,
Desperate to own you,
The drumming sound of a bull frog,
Seeks to nest in my own home.

I lost my home,
I lost my child,
For reasons I never knew,
I scrimped and saved for my loving home,
The impurities of a scum rose above,
My sweat and tears,
And possessed my priceless home.
Now it sits on my verandah,
Looking all innocent and chum,
Someone's hard work,
Just squandered away,
Because of a raving headless tramp,
Swindle and the cheat,
Sit together and partying in my home,
While I watch in the dark.
Social outcast I have become,
While the muttering mutt,
Sitting on my sofa,
Snoring away.

Shock of surprise,
The startling fact,
The true statement I seek,
Clouded mind of a lout,
Got my home in his palm,
The persistent sting of a stranger,
The twisted tales of a twin headed dumb,
I now recognise the drama of the scum,
I am wake,

My mind is clear,
I will get that swindler,
My dad is gone,
The yellow canary will be in my palm,
I swear and I curse,
But I know I'll get that,
Swindling tramp.

Bakthi Ross

<u>Sleeping Seal</u>

Sleeping seal,
Sealed in an emotion of peace,
Sleeping mind at peace,
Peaceful mind, Peaceful sleep.

World would never be in peace,
Like the sleeping seal,
Seal on a piece of paper,
Would never make that peaceful world.

We go to war and fight for that peace,
We make laws to reinstated that seal of peace,
If you are peaceful within yourself,
The world would be in peace.

We can move the mountains,
Divide the boundaries of a nation,
If you are not in peace within yourself,
All these laws and boundaries would be.
Meaningless.

To be in peace,
You have to be self-satisfied in what you are,

And what you have achieved,
Rather than wanting what others have and achieved,

If peace makers peace offerings,
To cloud the minds of the gullible,
World would be never be in peace,
There would be a war for this reason,
And for that reason,
There would be many little wars,
In every corner of the world.
If you are capable of making war,
You should be capable of making peace,
Lingering wars achieves nothing,
If you are capable of creating nature,
Like the God,
You have the right to destroy it,
It is easy to destroy but it is hard to create.

It takes time to create,
It does not take time to destroy it,
Skillful war achieves peace quickly,
A mindless was lingers and creates destructions,

If there is no peace after the war,
That was is a war of greed and destructions,
It is easy make war,
It is hard to hold that peace,
If peace makers really want peace,
We would not have any wars.

Some say there is no peace without war,
Then after the war we should have peace,
That is not a proven fact,
Because World War two did not restore peace,
Because one's beliefs and one's expectations of the world,
If you could change everyone according to one's beliefs,

And one's expectations,
One expects that world would be at peace.

If one sees the world as all white,
Then one's expectation is clouded,
He or she should see the world in black and white,
And accept that world will always have its problems.

No matter how many wars you fought,
And how many peace you make,
After a while you will find some other faults,
And you will go and fight another war.

It could be Lenin,
It could be Hitler,
It could be George Bush,
All looking for that self satisfaction,
And expecting the world to comply,
And help achieve their dreams.

If you are really looking for peace in the world,
You will satisfy majority of the world's expectations,
If is limited to one person's ideals and one society's progress,
Then you could expect another was in a few years time.

If you support koala species and didn't support the gum trees,
Then you will destroy both,
Everything in the world have some function towards the world,
Otherwise it would not exist in the world,
If you want the world to be bald and beautiful,
Then Tasmanian devil has no place in the world.

There is no peaceful world,
There is no paradise,
There is no perfect world,

There is no perfect leader,
There is no perfect government,
There is no perfect person,
You make changes that are constructive,
You accept the unchangeable things as facts of life.

If peace is a structured plan,
You will not achieve it,
Human nature is that they will,
Always complain about something,
Peace comes from within,
No wars, No amounts of money,
Will bring that peace upon the world,
If individuals are in peace,
The world would be in peace.

World is a sleeping seal,
Please do not disturb it.

By Bakthi Ross

Morning Glory

When the sun shines upon you,
You smile like the morning glory,
When the sun sets upon you,
You hold yourself close like a morning glory,
Your life has been a shining glory,
Like the morning glory,
When lightning struck,
You shut yourself down,
Like the morning glory,

When you are happy,
You lighten up,
Like the morning glory,

You are a shining light,
For others,
Like the morning glory,

When the darkness set upon us,
You are warm as the morning glory,

Happiness and sadness,
Like the day and night,
You conquered us morning glory,
We have learnt the life's ups and downs,
And shared the moments of good and bad times,
Like the morning glory,

By Bakthi Ross

Life

Life is short,
Make it fun,
Don't wait until you are done.

Life has its problems,
Keep it positive and carry on,

Have your fun,
Change your life,
Sing along and say your prayer,
For the life that was given.

Whatever it is,
Enjoy the days of your life.

Bakthi Ross

There Is No Sky

If there is no sky where will be the stars?
If there is no sky where will be planets?
If there is no sky there is limit,
It wouldn't be the infinite universe.

If there is gravity hour heads will be spinning,
If there is gravity our heels will be off the ground,
If there is gravity we will be dancing like the rotating planets,
If there is gravity we will fly like the birds,
And enjoy that endless feelings of motion.

When there is no end we love our enjoyment,
When there is no end we control our sadness,
When there is no end we create that limit,
Because we never could reach that end.

By Bakthi Ross

Motherhood

Quietness is quite comforting when the baby is sleep,
A baby's scream is deafening,
And I feel noisome,
Shss! Shss! I said to the other kids,
And I yell out and said "Keep quiet,"
Kids are smart and they take advantage of my situation,
They come one after another and whisper "Can I have this,
Can I have that,"
Sleeping baby in my hand and I am dreading for that peace,
I nod my head like a noddy but I am no fool.

I need that rest, I need that peaceful time,
I give in here a bit and I give in there a bit,
They take advantage of me, but I know that is what,

Makes me a mum.

I know them well still I couldn't say no,
Sometimes I give in and sometimes I tell them off,
If I give in I am a bit tired,
When I hear that little voice calling "Mum,"
I forget all about the stress of being a mum,
I do it all over again,
Mum! Mum! Motherhood is so fun, fun.

Bakthi Ross

<u>The Magic Words</u>

If you are busy	make some time,
If you are angry	calm down,
If you are dirty	clean yourself,
If you are smelly	change your diet,
If you are a bully	get over your problems,
If you are bossy boot	go to a management class,
If you are over the hill	be cynical,
If you are tired	go to bed,
If you are bored	bug your friend,
If you are a nag	stop complaining,
If you are happy	Just smile,

If "if," is what you are, make it what you could be.

Bakthi Ross

<u>Carpet Python</u>

Python! Python! Carpet Python!
Caboolture is the home of python,
Colourful trees and colourful skies,
Come and see the beauty of Caboolture,

Lakes and rivers,
Pelicans and swans,
Makes the day peaceful and pleasant,
Come and enjoy the time in Caboolture.

Spend a day! Spend a week!
Smell the fresh air of the special place,
Meet the people,
And make your day fun and happy.

Crabs and prawns,
Steaks and chips,
Salads and spaghetti,
Chinese and Indians,
Enjoy the tastes of Caboolture,
Because Caboolture welcomes you.

Bakthi Ross

<u>Douglas</u>

Douglas dude wanted a feud,
He hated the world,
He hated the land,
He was made to live.

He wages a war against the world,
He wanted to punish the world,
"His loyalty and devotion to his country,
No longer important," he said.
His duty is to take revenge.

Douglas dude's service to his own mind,
A deadly hatred,
He jumped to his insanity,

He made a bomb,
And became inflamed.

He would not be held accountable,
The devil! The demon!
He took the lives of many,
His unreliable mind,
Made him do this barbaric act.

If you could rely on your own mind,
Douglas dude would not have charred himself,
The demonic power!

Bakthi Ross

Paper Capital

Paper men! Paper men!
Place your bid on a takeover,
Bids are high, shares are low,
Save it from the liquidator.

Paper capital, paper liability,
Playing field for the paper men,
Books are fine,
Tax has no fines,
Takeovers makes up for the paper world.

Brought it forward,
Carried it down,
Paper balances kept them in business.

Monthly statements,
Yearly reports,
Made many millionaires,

Until the auditor said,
You have covered all the loop holes in the law,
But you have forgotten that time is the essence,
Of your paper assets and paper capital,
Now is the time to close the doors,
And burn all the papers.

Now you can say to your mates,
Once I was a millionaire,
And sit at home and repeat it over and over again,
Until your wife say not that same old story again,
And walks out on your life.

You can start again and be successful,
But you will know paper capital is not the way to be,
Unless you capitalise it on time.

But the materiality of the problem now assessed,
And you can be wiser,
And not bend the rules,
And cook the books,
A successful business is all about,
Timely funding,
Timely adjustments,
Time to promote,
And time to make a profit.

By Bakthi Ross

The Disease

It was not a monsoon,
It was not a cyclone,
It was not an earth quake,
It was a share market crash.

It was not a disease,
But it was contagious,
It infected the whole global share markets.

There were safety margins,
There were reserves,
There were disaster provisions,
There were insurance,
There were budgets and financial reports,
But somehow these plans didn't save the share market crash.

We assess our investment risks,
We create long and short term investments,
We predict the future fluctuations,
We also predict the natural disasters.

Then why there was a share market crash,
Did we forget to assess the market demand?
Or did we flood the market to push the other players out,
If there wasn't any demand will flooding of a market work?

If there is a debit there is always a credit,
You make money or you lose money,
Then why do the share investors are always in the losing end,
Am I stupid or you think I am?
Investors had to have this incurable disease,
Share market crash every now and then.

If it is a long term investment in the developing world,
You didn't assess the demands,
You didn't assess the risks of the long term investments,
You came stuck when the natural disaster hit,
You didn't have a provision,
Your insurance was inadequate.

You have computers, calculators and softwares,

To assess all the data,
You didn't allow for technology changes,
You have all the books that was written about investments,

You have a financial Planners,
You have economists,
You have accountants,
You have auditors,
You know all the company laws,
How come you cannot stop the share market crash?
And have that timely assessment,
When hyped up, inflated share prices hit the glass ceiling,
You come unstuck again.

Long term investments! Long term investments!
There is no structural risk assessment you can calculate,
You increase the share prices,
With your predictions that has no substance,
You hyped the minds of people with fancy advertising,
If your advertising looks good,
As the thin pin stripe suite you wear,
Then all your predictions are based on that thin line,
Then why do you call it "it fluctuates,"

You take that disaster provisions and you play with it,
And you expect others when disaster strikes to deal with it,
It is like the woollies you wear when you are cold,
You pull the wool over everyone's eyes,
When the crunch time comes,
you present us with another bill,
But this time it is the "Mental health bill,"

Share market crash is not inevitable,
Reality of share prices needs to be reported,
And assessed,
If there is a fake increase to attract market players,

That should be addressed,
Investors' capital should be protected.

Capital reserve,
Compulsory provisions,
Adequate insurance,
May save the world of that curable disease,
Called "Share Market Crash,"

By Bakthi Ross

Down But Not Out

Life is a rollercoaster,
When you tried to overcome the hurdles,
You jump three feet up,
But you come down a foot.

Never totally out,
Never totally successful,
You plod along day by day,
With that hope one day you'll…

You try harder and harder,
Some days you are totally out,
Some days you have some success,
That gives you that hope.
Holding on to that shred of hope,
Makes you want to wake up in the morning,
You write and you write,
A satisfaction of finishing a book,
Gives you that courage,
When you sent that manuscript to the publisher,
You wait for that rejection letter,
Now you are down for a day.

You read and you write,
You go to workshops,
You go to writer's groups,
So you would not feel totally down.

You are improving every day,
Even though publisher's contract is far from coming,
You know everything about,
Writing, publishing and marketing,
You have up-skilled yourself in your field,
You are no longer that gullible,
First time author.

Your life is a rollercoaster,
Some days you up with some,
Encouragements from others,
Other days you think about,
Whether to give up or carry on.

Then you see the books in the library,
Then you compare your work with others,
Now you say to yourself,
I am improving,
I'll get a publisher soon.
You keep sending manuscripts to publishers,

With some encouragements,
You feel down but not out.

By Bakthi Ross

www.ingramcontent.com/pod-product-compliance
Lightning Source LLC
Chambersburg PA
CBHW041522090426
42737CB00037B/5